Breakfast at
Wetherspoons

Breakfast at
Wetherspoons
Jim Greenhalf

Smokestack Books
1 Lake Terrace, Grewelthorpe, Ripon HG4 3BU
e-mail: info@smokestack-books.co.uk
www.smokestack-books.co.uk

ISBN 9781999827632

Smokestack Books
is represented
by Inpress Ltd

for Lesley

'the effect of her being on all around her was incalculably diffusive; for the growing good of the world is partly dependent on unhistoric acts; and that things are not so ill with you and me as they might have been is half-owing to the number who lived faithfully a hidden life...'

George Eliot, *Middlemarch*

Contents

One Man's Meat

One man's gain
is another man's loss.
One man's fool
is another man's boss.
One man's raft
is another man's cross.
One man's gold
is another man's dross.

One man's sword
is another man's plough.
One man's 'can't'
is another man's 'how?'
One man's beef
is another man's chow.
One's man's lie
is another man's vow.

One man's love
is another man's pain.
One man's drought
is another man's rain.
One man's bond
is another man's chain.
One man's blood
is another man's stain.

Poetry

The contriver of verses is a taxidermist.
Better a live sparrow than a dead eagle,
said Edward Fitzgerald, defending
his version of Omar Khayyam.
The Rubiyat was not a literal translation,
he added, simply a form
stuffed from his own, worse, life.

A Piece of Toasted Cheese

Much as I might want to take you
to Holy Island or to bed,
we'd only end up sore or sorry.

You are too smart to be that disingenuous;
I don't believe you, he said.
Self-serving narratives are rarely true.

Spare me the re-sprayed explanations.
Not since Jesus, Cicero or Rumi
has the human narrative changed.

Trivialities make the biggest difference –
bacteria in a petri dish, an icy runway,
a night to remember or the longest day.

Breakfast at Wetherspoons

St Paul's clocktower
would be a perfect sightline

for sniper-fire of the kind
she furtively directs.

Her ripostes are dumdum
bullets angled at the heads

of the eaters of Eggs
Benedict, the mixed grill,

the full English, splattering
those hunched over

brown Windsor tables,
eyes on the racing, fingers

tracing numbers in spillage.
They do not spy her

hooded, swivelling eyes
calculating the trigonometry,

as she loads another word
into the breach for firing.

Ready to go to work,
she has messengers to delete.

My Last Easter in Ilkley

You can read the Sunday papers all day long,
or plug your ears into mountain music from Peru.
Riddlers of pan-pipes, harps and guitars,
probably are humbler and more true

than those who empty car boots
at the municipal waste depot.
Rain dripping from the cross at the top of The Grove,
car boots filling again at Tesco.

The elderly talking with prayer books and Bibles.
A barista abused by one of the righteous.
Another frees charity boxes from their chains.
No big green bins for human detritus.

Friday Hill

This afternoon Christ died for me again.
Every year it happens.
Every year I forget.
I do not know why.

Faced with the Star Chamber of King Henry or King James,
I would be stumped to explain
powered flight,
the internal combustion engine,
or Thomas Crapper's plumbing.
Civilisation is as much a mystery to me
as women's hats,
Shane Warne's leg-break bowling,
or the Second Coming.

If I were Jesus,
I wouldn't die for me,
bent on nails on Friday Hill.

Among the Struldbrugs

Tired eyelids claw-hammered open
by early morning crows and jackdaws.
The metal shutters of the bakery rattling up.
The milkman clinking Bluetops,
waking the elderly couple below me.
He'd got cancer,
his wife another morning
of not being a widow.

Empty bottles waiting to be
taken, crated and carted away.
The curtailed warbling of wood pigeons
reminding me, Monday to Friday,
daily bread waited
to be earned and eaten.

Whether or not you've a job to go to,
time to get up and get moving,

Satnav for Lovers

We arranged to meet at Kings Cross.
In spite of delays and cancellations,
I made it to my destination.
Love had chosen to wait.

After forty years of drifting, eddies,
bridges burned or crossed,
we confounded expectation
and each other.

Water resounds to the impact of a stone:
that's how you dropped into me,
no longer in abeyance.
The canal is as straight and narrow as I am,

the river's current is unpredictable, as you are.
And for you they'll say
you're in at the deep end,
out of your depth, too far over your head.

And sometimes I lose the way.
In spite of all I think I know,
the thunder, the lightning,
the rain and the snow.

In spite of myself,
I lose the words, the feeling,
as I lose belief or sleep.
I give it up, I let it go.

There are no evident tracks to follow.
But words and feelings rekindle.
The twining clematis, dying,
comes back during winter.

In the Queue at the Co-Op

with Lesley Thorndyke

We met at the vegetables.
'Fray Bentos pies,' she said,
'two for three pounds.'
Her face was small and wizened,
with bright blue eyes.
She wore a funfair jacket, leggings
and a pair of fake crocs.

She said her name was Maguerite.
She said she came from Wales.
And when she went to bed
she liked to look at the night sky
above Mount Snowden,
to see what dawn would bring.

Both husbands were dead.
'But I didn't kill them,'
she told me twice.
Her doctor told her to eat, eat.
'I was down to four stone,' she said.
'Then you must,' I said.

I didn't see anyone listening.

2 March 2011

The Shelf Life of a Crisp

A crinkled membrane,
like a pharoah's ear;
entombed in an air-tight bag:
its fate is usually cut and dried.
The shelf-life of an average crisp,
whether baked or fried,
is four months, five months,
no more than six.
Slightly longer than a foetus
in the land of potato-eaters.

Though we have had but half
the time of an average crisp,
our fate is neither transparent nor opaque.
The shelf-life of our love,
pan-fried or half-baked,
depends on us.

Though Roses Please Her

as the odd green bottle of red,
or a weekend in Whitby or Paris,
none of this lights up her green eyes
as much as an Irwin Vise Grip,
a 36 pc Plumbing Kit
with tap rings;
better still a Draper 40-piece
rachet screwdriver set.

'I should have been an engineer,'
she says, setting my rented house to order.
Broken window latches have been replaced.
The bathroom wall supports a cabinet.
Heaven is a spirit-level, step-ladders
and a Power Craft hammer drill.

'And when I'm through,' she says,
reaching for her Wilko Toolbox saw,
'I'm going to start on you.'

The Usual Piddling Impedimenta

What woman, worthy of the noun,
would want to accommodate my surly, bachelor habits?
And what about my size, my silence, my sadness
my thinning hair and crooked teeth?

You're my love, she said, I don't care.
I hate the women you have known,
they made you unhappy,
I should have been there, she said.

At night, kneeling on the bed,
she creamed the hardened soles of his feet,
taking each vein-broken ostrich hoof
tenderly in both hands.

She kissed him in the kitchen,
smiled at him through her glasses,
poked his ribs on trains and always
stood in front on escalators going up.

His golden girl, his golden goose,
in spite of age's perfunctory, piddling impedimenta.
And when she returned from her travels
he met her with shepherd's pie, home-made.

Unspoken Conversations

The fate of words is
to emulate the river.
I had seen her there before,
the Asian woman by the weir,
rapt in a greyhooded shawl,
watching the water go over.

Police posters faded
on lamp-posts and trees.
A body washed up
nine miles away and I flinched,
shamed by the figure
of a drowning thought.

She had hired an afternoon taxi
to take her from roads and rooms.
She had a secret to keep
and disappeared like footprints
across a snow-black wood.
Would talking have helped?

They tried to fathom her,
all those unspoken conversations.
The river she embraced
swept her away and then forgot.
Each day is an unopened letter
behind the Town Hall clock.

Roses

Don't forget to smell the roses,
he used to say.
I never knew
what to reply.
For if roses grew
along my thorny way,
I never stopped
to smell them.
After that fatal
afternoon in May,
the roses
that bloomed
along his way
reeked of fire and smoke,
flesh and blood.
The smell of them
followed him
to his desecrated grave,
and still do
today.

Crown Shyness

In one hectare of the Matto Grosso
there is more diversity
than Hong Kong or Mexico City.
Seven hundred species of flora
compete for sunlight
yet flourish by avoiding entanglements.

Canopy observers,
paid to categorise such things,
call this behaviour
crown shyness.
Trees somehow get along
by ceding space to each other.

From the immensity of Saturn's earrings,
Earth's pale blue opal
is a pixel;
a drop in the black ocean of every eye,
that ever looked beyond the treeline of the galaxy
and wondered why.

Soufflés

'You remind me of a cook,' a friend said,
'trying to save a collapsed soufflé
by desperately stirring in
additional, stronger ingredients.'
That's me, that's you, that's anybody
trying to cook up poetry.

Doctor Johnson, whose appetite
for food and words was gluttonous,
gnawed the bone of what writing was for.
To make money, and help us
endure the pains of life
and enjoy its pleasure more.

Well, I've made a bit of money
and know the consolation of writing;
but whether poetry helps anybody
figure out the furtive motives
of fugitive Joel Cairo in the rank bazaar
of failed men, I do not know.

Horrible Year

If, for you, the good life started in 1963,
after the worst winter since '47
and The Beatles' Please, Please Me;
the Yom Kippur War and OPEC
put paid to that in 1973 –
after the currency was decimalised

and Heath sold out to the EEC.
Lord, protect
what little sovereignty
our state has left,
from those whose wit
exceeds their grace;

and from those
with neither grace nor wit,
whose actions lead us
into temptation,
or worse,
the shit.

Scotland's First Immigrants

The heavy metal Ninth Legion
must have liked the climate
beyond the walls of York.

The food and native friendliness too
must have made a change
from orders, decimation and pork,

because not one of them,
more than five-and-a-half thousand
armed and armoured men,

came back across the border.

A Work in Progress

Our little systems have their day.
They have their day and cease to be.
Tennyson's lines from In Memoriam
come to mind as coastal rollers

glisten the backs of distant dolphins.
On a tilted flight-deck of sea-rinsed rock,
the half-sunk torso of some old god,
we watch them stitch together the tartans

of the Moray Firth. The Medusa lighthouse opposite
tries to fix the future in stone.
But the limestone blocks
we stand upon, nude grey and salmon pink,

like the pigs above Hopeman's Harbour Street,
alter under seawater's hammer and chisels.
A work in progress, like us,

we like to think.

Snail on a Red Hot Poker

Lager at twenty

an agar at thirty

Prada at forty

a Lada at fifty

Saga at sixty

After Eights

at seventy

after which

gaga

probably.

Culloden

From a distance it looks like a golf course in Brobdingnag:
tee-green places marked by blue flags and red flags
ten to twelve feet high, cracking in squalls
like plastic shopping bags
snagged on hawthorn hedges.
But these are not fairways for lost golf balls:
the flags denote the places where Charles Stuart's ploy
was scotched by Redcoat grapeshot and musket balls.
Rocks lodged among heather and sedge
on Drummossie Moor
mark the bunkers of the dead.

On Looking Down into Water

Surprising myself I organised a weekend in the capital of love:
a hotel on the boulevard de Bonne Nouvelle
and a Manet retrospective at the Musee d'Orsay.
Floating under the bridges of Paris on the Friday,
walking over Pont Alexandre III the next.
Looking down, once again I resisted the temptation

to fling everything in – coat, passport, identity –
and sink or swim like Jack Nicholson
in Five Easy Pieces. Or Reginald Perrin.
According to Desert Island Discs
all any soul needs is a few isolated acres,
eight records and three books:

no income, no outcomes, no football, no love.
Sod that. I couldn't be a Filipino compressor fisherman,
sucking on a leaky garden hose thirty metres deep,
nor a refugee on a raft of phones.
We walked away from Manet's bearded men of property
in pursuit of life, liberty and happiness.

Scarecrows

The photograph shows
the stuffing coming out of them.
Botox grimaces,
xylophone teeth.
Pitted
like cherries,
cored
like apples,
prunes.
Men of the Commune
racked and arrayed
in knocked together boxes
shaped like lozenges.
Shabby boots,
scraggy coats,
hands crossing their heart
or the place
where love had been,
bayoneted
or shot.
Gallic cocks
no longer crowing.

Another One Falls

They've all got guns and designer shades
and skid about hot ruined streets
in odd ensembles of Mad Max vehicles
scrawled with swooping script.

For the benefit of television news
they shoot from the hip, from bearded lips,
firing prayers and bullets into the blue.
The Lewis Carroll dowager

whom they toppled and killed
proves, once again,
that nothing, good or bad,
outlives people's willingness to believe in it.

Crowns And Bridges

Such is the grimness of the times
we must wear a brave face
they tell us and, though the brain is bleeding,
smile. So I went the extra mile,
eight hundred or more,
to a little town in Hungary,
far poorer than my own.

Along a road like a pre-war centre parting,
a doctor-dentist in lime-green crocs
looked into my mouth as though
sounding the wobbly keys
of an old, stained piano.
He played my teeth with his fingers,
tuning their soundness.
The loose and crooked he replaced.
Eleven others he hollowed like bullets,
capping gun-metal grey amalgam
with white acrylic.

Forty years before in Budapest,
colleagues hoping for richer fillings
had ventured West.
This mender of shy smiles and crooked teeth,
fluent in Hungarian, French and German,
was content where he was.
The poor paid him in chickens,
vegetables and crops.
I paid him in cash.

He popped the stopper from a bottle
and dropped peach-flavoured rocket fuel
into a small lidded pot,
a relic of the Hapsburg empire
before the First World War
blew away crowns and bridges.

Statues in Budapest

Once again they have been placed on pedestals:
incredible hulks of granite and bronze.
Out of obscurity in Memento Park,
waiting for history or Ray Harryhausen
to make them miraculous.

Arms raised in permanent semaphore,
as though warning the future
they are waiting to march once again.
The toppled prophets and apostles
who commissioned them

have less purpose than a Rubik's Cube,
or so it seems, while we
twist and turn our various pieces to make them fit.
Turning and twisting, trying to connect
with something
        out of alignment.

Hungary in March

A neighbouring farmer
made his way as a KGB major.
Bred Mangalitsa pigs
on three hundred acres.
Exhibited weapons and Nazi uniforms.
Governments paid him to advise them
on counter-terrorism.
Locals showed their respect
by not asking questions.

A pump and a yellow bucket,
Axe-heads swelling in weeded water.
Lopped cylinders of acacia logs
waiting like heads to be chopped.
Imprisoned spring rises underfoot.
Stars come out more brightly
when sensors are off.
Under the bright claws of the Bear
killer dogs laugh like foxes.
Nights are cold but clear.

Spam

Spam, ham, Speenhamland:
words of school dinners,
homework and exams.
Spam was what he used to eat.
The swishing steel wheel of a red guillotine
planed it into tissue-thin slices,
folded in squares of grease-proof
by the grocer, Champ,
a small, balding, spritely man
who wore a brown linoleum coat.
He did not know that spam was invented,
a poor man's ham, a stand-in.
Only girls were taught cookery in the Sixties.
He did not ask why.
                              His mother filled his plate
with rock eel and especially skate,
pork, corned beef and spam.
She did two jobs to pay the rent
and feed her only son steak,
while she ate bubble-and-squeak
alone in the scullery.
                              He never asked why.
In spite of all the food she fed him,
her son was a serial disappointer.
Just like your father, she said,
trying to make sense.
And just like his father, he too left home,
to pick the bones of experience.

Dissenters

In the years before
France's revolutionary wars,
John Wesley rode a horse
uphill to Baildon moors.
Steep Browgate is now revved
by ten tonne buses and four-by-fours
to the round-about where
quarrymen and weavers
congregated outside a chapel door.
They came to hear
the Bible man tell them
of love's holy connexion,
and why they should endure.

Whose cup spills over?
The emptiest pots make the loudest din.
Clay is stronger when it's fired,
flesh is stronger when it's hired.
Look through a glass darkly:
half-empty or half-full?
Some have no glass at all,
others no water,
no country.

Food Of Love

Man is born free and everywhere he is in chainstores.

Scattered about Shakespeare's bust in Love Lane,
boxed bones, bits of skin and flesh.
Eucharist of love's lunchtime remains,
an Alpha Romeo lying to Juliet:
I love you more than Golden Nuggets
and all the Whoppers in the world.

Only the young dream of consummate fucks.
Love, unlike enriched uranium, is not all-consuming
for those obliged to scrape a crust.
Drink to me only if you must;
but first let me feast on breasts and thighs and legs.
Then, like that love-sick arse Orsino,
cushioned by banks of unearned income,
I too might dream of ultimate head.

Given a choice between a loaf and thou,
I think I'd pick the bread.

The Man on the 17:11 to Skipton

All women are beautiful, in their own way,
sang the florid-faced shambler to the man
sitting opposite on the 17:11 to Skipton.
He plunked an imaginary guitar.
I am an angel. I am. An angel, he sang,
beating time with a pocket bottle of Scotch.
One of the fallen or just a local old soak,
obliterating bleak February
in a boozy stupor.

For two stops my mood lightened.
Our burgled home – the things taken,
the time stolen – was forgotten.
I suppose he's happier in his little world
than we are in ours, one of the beautiful said
at Frizinghall, getting off,
as the angel, on the 17:11 to Skipton,
plunked an imaginary guitar,
a half bottle of Scotch at the ready.

Is That What it's Really Like?

You have a day when everything goes the way
you hoped or planned.
Rain that was forecast did not wash away
serendipity with the commuting sun.
Everything you tried came off.
No hell or Helen or bills to pay.
At one with nature,
the universe,
Leonard Cohen,
Richard Dawkins,
Kendo Nagasaki.

It's only when tooth-ache, heart-ache,
or one of the plagues of Egypt,
strikes, when something sticks in your back,
your heart, your throat;
words somebody says
you said or wrote;
it's only when bills flood in
and money dries up;
when your car or computer breaks down
or somebody breaks in;
when your mother, sister or brother
drops out or goes missing;
when the consultant calls you in;
when the dog in the manger
kills the baby,
or the cat
eats the albatross:

only then,
if you still believe life is beautiful,
does it make a difference.

Jihadi John

The black-masked executioner
carved his knife
into the kneeling man's neck
the way our old boot-mender
pulled the curved
trimming blade towards
his stained apron chest.

Now innocence must be proved;
Habeas Corpus is no longer a fact;
on the hooded authority of courts,
the body is dead-headed.

The gods of Greece and Rome,
warned us before they disappeared
what happens when the love of life
is overpowered by the love of death.

Assemble bugles' broken tubes,
summon dead squaddies' body parts
to shires they would not recognise.
Pile up the coastal pyres,
Flamborough to Beachy Head.
This night
will not close those eyes.

The Old Man of Palmyra

Khaled al-Asaad, 82
murdered by ISIS, 18 August 2015

It meant nothing to me, the Old Testament
temple, a dollar attraction,
blown up in sand-coloured pillars of smoke
by men in black.
The old man of Palmyra
wasn't among the refugee rivers
running from war and ruin,
the men in black.

They came looking for idolatrous antiquities
to smash them or flog them
for more engines of ruin and war.
Faith greater than his fear, the old man,
who could have told the masked men
where to find the treasures
they were counting on,
chose to remain.

He chose to say nothing.
They chose to end him like John the Baptist,
roping him headless to a post.
They blew up the temple.
Some were shocked. I was not.
It meant less to me than the old man's
love, his refusal.

Old Men Have Braces, Young Men Have Belts

with Michael Stewart

Young men wear belts,
old men wear braces.
Young men wreck slip-ons,
old men save laces.

Young men are bearded,
old men bear creases.
Young men sport trackies,
old men share fleeces.

Young men are fickle,
old men capricious.
Young men are know-alls,
old men suspicious.

Young men are violent,
old men are spiteful.
Young men are fearful,
old men are frightful.

Old men say nothing's
new under the sun.
But young men feel older
now, colder and done.

Reflections on The Demolition of Clarence Flour Mill, Hull

So this was where they
milled the grain
that made the bread
that kept fishermen
and their families fed.
And this was the river,
brown and silted now,
where ships came in
and, loaded with bales,
sailed out again.

And this was the smithy
where manacles were made
that shackled the wrists
and ankles of slaves.
The smith who made them
thanked God, probably,
grateful for the work,
the money, the opportunity
to chain the future
for his family.

Just do your job
and go away,
thankful
if what falls on you
is only water.

The Mantis Shrimp

It punches harder than Mike Tyson,
moves faster than Usain Bolt,
and its sixteen photoreceptors see more
than David Hockney's nine cameras,
mounted on a four-by-four
to photograph different angles simultaneously.

Its god is light and colour.
In its underwater world it is a four-inch panzer.
Exotic, robotic, a lunar module
drawn by Dan Dare's Frank Hampson,
or Yellow Submarine's Heinz Edelmann.
It mines a bolt hole in coral.

Unlike homo saps,
it does not make a mess where it loves.
Greed, lust and murder
are beyond it.
It does not kick sand in the face of passing molluscs.
It kills to feed and breed.

Diogenes

Sometimes I think Diogenes was right:
we are tossing in spittle,
ever closer to the lip of the falls.

Between the art of the cooper,
the butcher, the baker, the undertaker,
civilisation totters or prospers.

And every so often
somebody barrels over Niagara,
to measure his mettle, his bottle, his balls.

No More Novenas

Every year they do it.
Every Christmas they pay for
nine New Year novenas,
and me not even a Catholic.
And every year, after the ninth day,
misfortune follows.

Last year illness lingered until Spring.
The year before that,
the economy collapsed.
This year burglars broke in
and stole the Bank of England.
Now there are bailiffs at the door,
revenue marshals at the gate
and everywhere, sleeping policemen.

So I'm asking, please,
no more novenas.
If bad luck is my lot,
pray only that I don't
bore everybody
luckier.

No More Excuses

Lord Byron saw Lady Wilmot Horton
and said she walked in beauty,
like the night. The maid in peace with all below,
had skid marks on her drawers,

as did Cecelia Gallerani,
Leonardo's painted Lady with the Ermine,
as I have on mine, sometimes,
as you have on yours.

Wan dolls in indigo, wan dolls in gold:
all that glitters from lobes and wrists:
the apple of the arse defined by a thong:
love without mammograms and menopause.

Lord B's heart gave out at thirty-nine,
though love was not the cause that killed him.
No more excuses, I said at sixty.
Still finding out what that means at sixty-four.

Aberystwyth

Slicker than a stage magicians's sleight of hand,
a breeze covered the valley with cloud
and, for a while, the land of hallucinatory
high hedges, Welsh cakes and poets,
was obscured by desultory piddle.

It lifted and drifted out to sea.
We followed it down to the town,
past the Ebeneezer chapel,
the Chip Box and windy Spar,
over the grey road bridge
squatting on miner's heels,
to the South Pier.

There the coin-shoving machine,
a pan-handler sifting for gold,
added to its slag heaps of silver and copper.
Just another coin, boy, it seemed to sneer
as our windfall hopes of avarice
teetered on Niagra's edge.
We consigned our greed to the beach
where the shove-ha'penny tide
rinsed and sorted its change
between landmines of jellyfish,
whispering, *Hush love, never mind.*

From tall storeys of trees,
Red Kites, Aztec feathers
frosted Himalayan white,
spiralled heights
higher than we could spin
the moon or a ten pence piece.

Maurice Wilson

born 1898, Bradford; died 1934, Mount Everest

Off again. Gorgeous day:
his final legible entry; alone,
four miles or more on Everest,
sub-zero sanity. No valedictory,
no pitiful letter home.
He set out to reach the top on his own.

The 5,000-mile Gypsy Moth flight to India –
cockpit open to extremities,
onlypaper maps and a compass –
would have been enough;
but he had another world to conquer
beyond Kipling, Buchan, W E Johns.

Six thousand feet below
the summit's howling horn,
mountaineers found Wilson's body.
Whether he succumbed going up
or perished stumbling down,
the climbers could not say.

A Big White God

Especially the greatest have feet of clay –
Churchill, Enid Blyton, Mohammad Ali.
The bombastic conqueror of Liston,
Frazier and Foreman,
waited for his implacable god
to take him out.

When unsinkable Titanic went down for the count
like unbeatable Jack Johnson,
a big white god glided by.
The North Atlantic wrinkled, momentarily –
a towel thrown in –
then everything resumed exactly as before.

After the passage of a god,
a great white star, a war,
what remains?
Crosses mark battlefields and plots
where treasure and legends are buried.
The rest is prattle and drains.

The Death of Atlas

I

The weight of the world on his shoulders
sank the feet of Atlas
deep into the mud,
until all that could be seen of him
was the boulder
above.

II

I watched a man in a London street
trying to stand upright.
The harder he tried the more
his ironing-board legs kept collapsing.
His head hit the angle
of a garden wall rising to hurt it.
Each fall bloodier than the last.
Thicker than ketchup
smacked from a bottle,
blood gouted from his nose,
snotting his face with red.
Last time I looked over my shoulder,
he was pushing the world away
with his head.

III

A blue plaque above a former doorway
marks the spot where the homeless life
of Jimmy the Toothless Smiler
stopped falling.
For a year or two he came to rest at night
under the stone shoulder of the media museum,
an angle-poise moon
his light.
And all the stars that his eyes saw,
though dead, will never cease;
nor all the tented people
who pray for peace.

Kalo Taxidi

in memory of Sebastian Barker, poet and editor

Our hilly April woods are dusted with bluebells,
upright as Scots Guards or Paris dancing girls.
Kalo taxidi: have a good journey through them.
In the flowery mountains of the Peloponnese,
as banks crashed and the value of money burned,
he wrote his last poems and made his peace.

I met him when times were different:
a party at Christies to toast his editorship
of *The London Magazine.* Cheshire cat grin,
the wings of his hair dashed back,
a demeanour that beamed. Anything
was possible. We arranged to talk and eat,
a street near his North London home.
Hives of roasting meat on spikes,
Oregano, red wine, coffee,
aromas from the Bosphorus, the Aegean.
Then he was gone.

A scientist on television explained
that in quantum physics bi-location
is a common occurrence.
Kalo taxidi, my friend, *kalo taxidi*,
in London and in Greece.

The Harmony of Opposites

At thirty-two Tolstoy needed dentures.
That didn't stop him writing *War and Peace*.
Pyorrhea kissed off Clark Gable's teeth.
But that didn't stop Rhett Butler
wooing the Scarlett woman.
As for Frank O' Hara,
he drank alone in a bar on 42nd Street,
waiting for Edward Hopper
to paint him out of a corner.

Francis Egerton,
third Duke of Bridgewater,
washed his hands of love
and threw himself into canals.
However much I'd like to believe
in the harmony of opposites,
the iron bridge and the rainbow
cannot be bolted together.
Yet the cyclamen outside our window
flourishes in inclement weather.
Unlike us, it is in the pink.

I am not a falcon circling a dove,
nor a cloud in trousers.
I'm an awkward sod,
going against the grain:
a misanthrope in love.

Everything Figures

Like prime numbers we are indivisible.
Proportion and harmony
figure in our multiples.
Despite the chaos of reality,

bread is baked, the dead are buried;
we take the weight, we share the load.
Averse to symmetry's perfection,
being contrary,
        unevenness pleases us better.

Wiping the Glass Clean

Every morning I passed the old man in his allotment.
Always solitary, rooting, digging slowly, planting,
unaware of me on my way to the station;
the mill's sign red above his gladioli spires
and tented strings of runner beans.
He became part of my morning,
like Steve, the municipal street cleaning man,
and the woman sweeping
behind the café-bar's tinted windows.

Job gone, no longer commuting, I lost sight of the old man;
but whenever routine took me down the hill
past his furrows, I looked out for him.
One morning of sleet and showers
ghost words on his greenhouse appeared:
RIP Joe.

Whoever painted them must have wiped the glass clean,
for when I passed his flowers again the words were
gone, as though the old man or my job
had never been.

Out of a Clear Blue Northern Sky

John Pashley 1934-2016

'I want to go now,' he said three times
on the last morning of his life.
The man who broke the boundaries
of his birth-right's expectations, flying
in cold war Coastal Command bombers,
closed his Royal Air Force blues and left
us behind. Wondering what we would do
without his hedgy eyebrows, the coffee
and cognac mornings in winter
and those Indian summer back-garden
afternoons of fruit trees and flowers,
peace and stability for hearts and minds.

Dyeing was his art, for nearly forty years
he helped to clothe a generation.
The fabric of his life was well-paid work
and mainly faithful loving, felting Cyn, his wife,
for thirty years through cancer.
Seven more as a widower,
cooking for family, friends and Sara,
sending stroppy letters to the shoddy press,
turning recovered oak and mahogany
into tables to give away.
The happiness of others his flight-path,
though, 'To thine own self be true,' I heard him say.

Weeds

World War 1 taught my grandmother's generation
how to roll a smoke under bombardment
and light a fire in a storm.

World War 2 taught my mother's generation
how to sleep underground
and know the difference between a rocket and a bomb.

Two generations had to make do and mend,
usually without men.
The twentieth century's last generation, my own,

grew out of control like ragwort, rosebay willow herb,
purple rhododendron. In goods yards and stations,
images of ugly beauty and desolation;

consolation of a kind.
Ideas take root in splits, fissures, fault-lines.
Successive wars taught me that weeds

are thrivers, tenacious survivors,
heart's ease for somebody,
amid monstrosities and ruins.

A Love Poem of Sorts

Shall I compare her to his Eighteenth Sonnet?
My love is not April, May, nor bursting June,
but Lesley Rose, whose summer's lease,

like my own, swells towards its sell-by date.
My fading rose smiles without vanity or cunning.
She tells me she loves me and I surprise myself

by saying so as well. Two cars, three freezers,
a mock-Tudor home, a dog, an annual income
double my own, she gave up for a rented life with me,

thirty years a solitary, in the twilight zone.
What the young Yevtushenko wrote in 'Breaking Up' –
True kindness in love means staying quite sober,

weighing each link of the chain you must bear.
Don't promise her heaven, suggest half-an-acre;
not 'unto death', but at least to next year –

should be set to music and sung at weddings,
the way Memento Mori was flung
into a triumphant Roman emperor's ear.

A bouquet of roses usually hides something vile.
These days love is not love without a publicist,
a confessional, or at least a slot on Jeremy Kyle.

We used to watch it in the gym on Sundays,
she on one treadmill, walking, me on another, praying.
Improbably, together again after forty summers.

Most Do Their Whimpering Long Before the End

The prayer rushes out,
over two thousand years,
borne on sea waves and air waves,
the church bell,
the parting knell;
from the sea bed,
the sick bed,
the monastery and prison cell,
death row and Rotten Row,
first breath and last breath;
under the hammer,
under the tanner,
the scythe
and the scanner,
the prayer rushes out;
a voice returning,
attuned to the song
of its own volition.

A Shared Life

The poet lost his way,
a man before he was a boy.
All men of stature have feet of clay
if they make success
the solitary measure of their happiness.
Bitter men die alone,
disillusioned with their choice,
crying into a glass, a cell or a phone.

It took a Fletcher from Leeds
to alter the flight of Eliot's arrow.
She was the bull's eye he hit,
not the Nobel Prize for Literature.
In spite of his world renown,
she helped him come into his own,
readied him for a shared life:
love, a wife, a home.

Ranter Remembered

in memory of Barry MacSweeney, poet and news editor of Bradford's Telegraph & Argus

We come trailing clouds of glory,
wrote the Lakeland laureate postmaster;
but MacSweeney, laurels of fire
enflaming his wine-red, blushful brows,
came trailing chains of fax paper,
dispatched from his suburb of hell;
his crooked face ballooning in the starry darkness,
mournful as a damaged moon.

He liked others to think he was on the ball,
up to the brim, ahead of the game.
He struggled, succumbed and died
between the thieves of praise and blame,
about the outcome still uncertain.
Alone among memos and empties,
cold as an un-ironed shirt, they found him
on a January morning.

On the shelves of Newcastle University
his life measures twelve yards –
the distance between goal-line and penalty spot,
St James' Park and the Infirmary.

Dante's Death Mask

Not the Gaze of the Gorgon,
but the long and studied stare
of Tony Harrison.
Under a rack of red television lights,
waiting to talk about his love
of rhyme and reason.

Prostate cancer at seventy-seven.
'Not good,' he said.
'There's still work for you to do,' I said,
the memory of his front-page poems
from Iraq and Bosnia still fresh
under the blackening blood shadow of Syria.

'There bloody is,' he said,
leaning forward for emphasis.
Undistracted by fear of hell or hope of heaven,
he sat, rock-like, on the make-shift stage;
Dante's death mask, his face,
waiting for questions.

As You May Not Like It

Come Jacques,
if, as you maintain,
all the world's a stage
and each of us a player
of many parts,
then all our play-acting,
on and off the page,
comes down to this:
does anyone
ever learn to act his age?

Hygga

In Danish it means being gentle on yourself.
If you are the centre of the universe,
smiling at the fool in the mirror makes sense:
cutting some slack instead of your throat.

I take the point. But gentleness, I've found,
is often a line flung out by anglers
whose anger management's deficient.
We'd all like to be loved

rather than judged or held to account;
but the Pennine climate's against
self-indulgence of the kind embraced by Danes.
Yorkshiremen do not like to be wrong –

footed or caught out by emotions,
the fishy chuggers of the heart.
The unreasoning milk of human kindness
may rust the mind, curdle the dream of consciousness.

More than forty Northern winters reeled me in:
so much storm-water over the weir,
so much debris snagging the bridge.
For more than forty years

I tried to stand in the current of events,
feel the flow under the surface,
the piking heron, conscience,
inspecting each darting wish.

Much as I like the idea of a saunter
in Copenhagen or Shangrila,
and though I am softer than Yorkshire's water,
hoo-ga? I wouldn't trust it.

That Was the Year

for Bob Light

1967 must seem like heaven now.
There was plenty of work
to go to or shirk.
No bombs in cars,
just dynamite in skirts.

Hard Days Night Hotel

For dreamers scheming on corners
or writing inside a shell;
for our ladies of the Mersey
with only a life to sell;
for love turned to stone on Hope Street,
between towers of heaven and hell;
it's the summer of love, the summer of blood
at the Hard Days Night Hotel.

Our backs to the wall with the writing
pretending that all is well,
as it was in the days before everything
rolled like a rock down a fell.
There's rain on Menlove Avenue
and a feeling that's hard to quell.
Revisit the days you lost touch with
at the Hard Days Night Hotel.

There's a storm blacking up in the distance
and somewhere the sound of a bell.
You're never too old for a saviour,
I heard a man say in a cell;
but don't expect any favours
if you've nothing to buy or sell.
Take a walk round the courts of Mathew Street
to the Hard Days Night Hotel.

Running

In the Sixties people wanted to be heavy.
Sumo wrestling had a brief vogue.
The Body Mass Index of enormous men,
Barry White, Demis Roussos, Pavaroti,
was the thing.
Rotundity was profundity.
Black was already beautiful,
then fat was beautiful too.

Now people run to be light.
Morning, noon and night,
Earth's tectonic plates reverberate
under the soles of pounding feet.
People used to walk and jog.
Now they run with attitude.
In the Eighties
Jane Fonda told them
to feel the burn.
Now they run
to stop themselves
burning out.

And I think:
Oh, for a little less of me
until, lithe and balding,
I can run high-headed like a Kenyan,
breathing more evenly,
sleeping more deeply,
as I used to.

Selfie on the Way to Surrey

That's me, at sixty-seven,
in the middle of Westminster Bridge.
Scudding clouds like gunpowder smoke
above Parliament between
the cross-hairs of the London Eye.
Yellow-jacketed police, male and female,
like television presenters in pairs,
pose with hosts of tourist selfie-takers
by dying kerbside daffodils.
Above the bra-line of the pregnant river,
the bald dome of St Paul's,
windy shards of steel and glass,
towers of money and towers of blood,
where men were burned for a book
and heads and newsprint rolled.

And the hanged man, under Blackfriars Bridge,
danced his lonely masque,
a telephone dangling, off the hook.
Brightness falls from the air
banking aircraft await a landing.
Everyone hoping blue chips will come in,
before another grey sunset docks
and the day seeks absolution or asylum.
England had music, freedom, the boys of Sixty-six.
Those days have gone.
Does anyone care or remember?
As long as I can walk over water,
pay my dues and make my way with one,
I have another future to share
north and south of the river.

In Passing

I remember thunder rolling
among Albania's mountains
and a sea-breeze cooling
Corfu's meat-heated night,
red wine and lightning.
And so great moments pass away
into the dim light of bathos.
We arrive uninvited,
sometimes unwanted,
without a visa or immunity.
What begins as a journey,
on the road, in the head,
mostly ends on a gurney.

This word is Latin,
that word is German,
those ones are French.
What is any of that to me?
I was raised on the Wheel of Fortune,
unfortified by men in cells.
O Boethius, O Bonhoeffer,
I cannot move, O Christ,
I cannot catch my breath.
We come from the land of bugger all
and bugger about in wind and rain.
Some do quite well, others go to hell.
Pilgrimage, quest or
Strictly Come Dancing,

it buggers us all the same.

Thinking Outside the Box

Whenever I am exhorted
to think outside the box,
usually by somebody
who should be in one,
I think of triple World Cup winner
Edson Arantes do Nascimento –
Pele.
Brazil's Black Pearl scored
twelve hundred and eighty-two goals
in thirteen hundred and sixty-three matches,
by not
thinking
outside the box.

Bubbly

My mother gave us bubbly from an early age.
We scooped it from a yellow crock
after the roast on Sundays.
Evaporated milk, fruit juice and jelly,
strawberry or lemon, melted in hot water,
hand-whisked, whipped thick and left to set.
Pinker than Zsa Zsa Gabor's lipstick.
The bowl upended over your head
proved true bubbly's worth.
Its pockmarked surface was like the moon's
seen from London E.17,
before Neil Armstrong put his space-boot on it.
Excavated dollops, scooped with a spoon,
were smoother than Mr Norris's corner-shop ice-cream,
plusher than West End cinema seats.
Bubbly kept me a while longer from running off
in pursuit of the dream.
If ever I find it or it finds me,
I'll not serenade the Milky Way
with flutes of Mumm, Moet or Verve-Cliquot:
I'll stick to fruitful scoops of bubbly
Lesley now makes for me.

Waiting for the Cats of the Ferryman

*in memory of David Tipton, writer, translator, editor, publisher
and gambler*

I thought I saw him in Barcelona,
glancing doubtfully upwards at Gaudi's spires.
He no longer rings in testy reaction to the news,
or to tell me something he told before.
He gave up swimming a mile a day,
cooking for friends and answering the phone.
Sitting out his days in a bare-boarded room,
smoking by the window, ear to the door,
rinsing his mouth with tinned foam,
the taste of brown Britannias on his tongue.
Waiting for the cats or the Ferryman
to fetch him home.

'A man who stands for nothing
will fall for anything.'
Malcolm X

Acknowledgements

Thank you to my friend the writer Michael Stewart for helping to choose the ingredients of this cook up. He once gave me a piece of advice I kept in mind while preparing this volume. 'Sometimes it is better to tell and sometimes it is better to show. A man losing a tooth makes me think about my mortality. Someone telling me to think about my mortality doesn't.'

Some of these poems were first published in *Pennine Platform* and in Michael Stewart (ed) *A Complicated Way of Being Ignored.*